Focus

The focus of this book is:

- to locate information on the page,
- to read for information.

 Tuning In

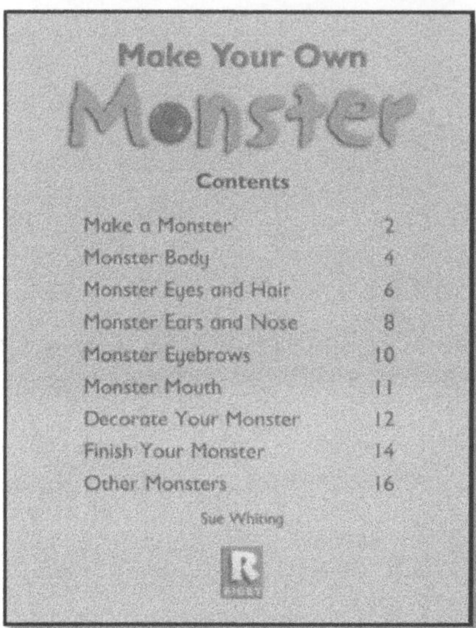

The front cover

Read the title and tell me what you think this book is about.

Speaking and Listening

You know how the writing would look on the page of a story book, how might this text be different?

The back cover

What does the blurb tell us about the book?

Contents

What information does this page give us?

Speaking and Listening

Will we need to start at the beginning or can we choose any page to start?

Tuning In

What do you think the information is on this page?

Speaking and Listening

Have you ever made a monster? What did you use to make it?

 ## Observe and Prompt

Word Recognition

- Check the children are reading words such as 'Monster' and 'plastic' confidently and are applying their decoding skills to more difficult words on these pages (e.g. 'coloured').

- Check the children can read the adjacent consonants using their blending skills (e.g. in the words 'tells', 'paint' and 'brushes').

- Prompt the children to read the sub-headings ('Tools' and 'Materials') as well.

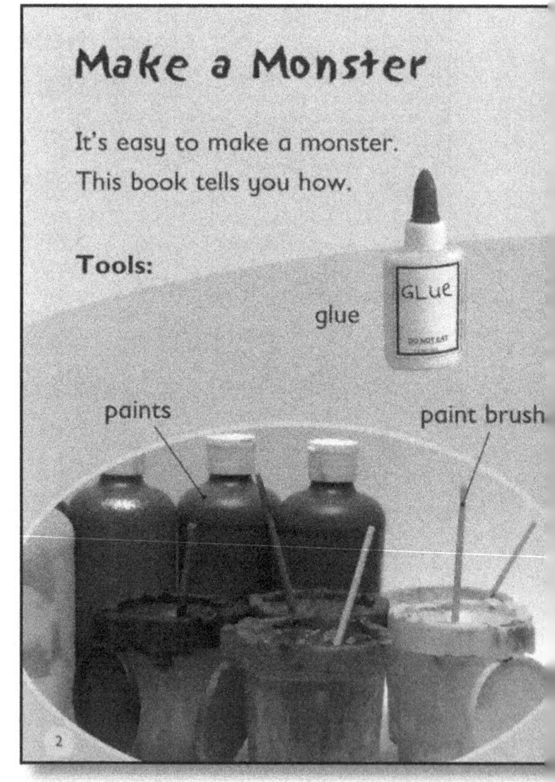

2

# Tuning In

Have you seen this before? (scouring pad) Where would you find it in the house? What do you think the boy will use it for?

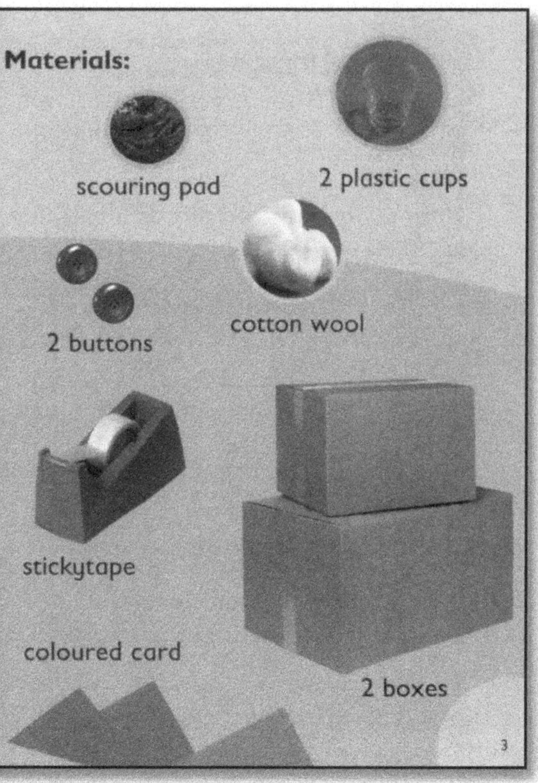

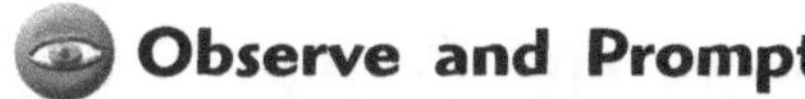# Observe and Prompt

Language Comprehension

- Ask the children what this book is going to help them do.

- Ask the children what tools they will need.

- Have any of the children ever made a monster before?

Tuning In

What do you think you will need to find first?

How will you make the box strong?

How will you use the small box?

 **Observe and Prompt**

Word Recognition

- Check the children can read the adjacent consonants at the beginning and end of words (e.g. 'First', 'flaps', 'strong', 'Glue').

- Check the children can use their decoding skills to tackle more difficult words, such as 'head', 'body' and 'small'.

- Prompt the children to break the word 'together' down into three syllables, before blending the whole word together.

4

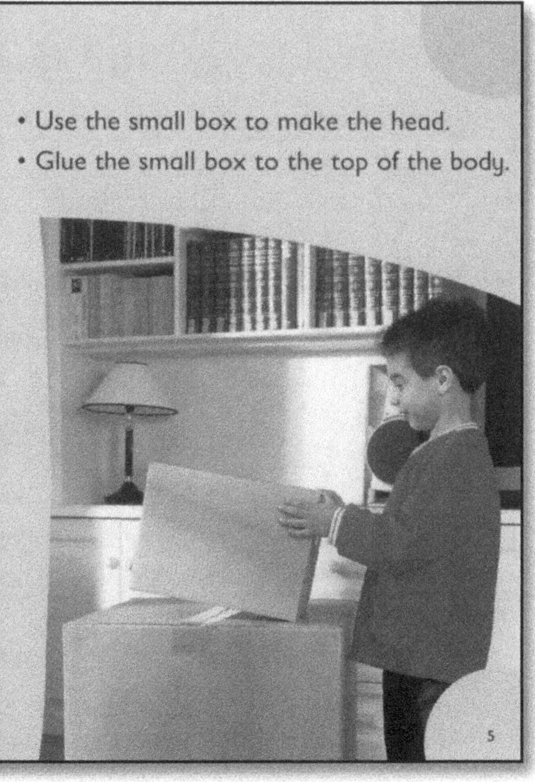

Observe and Prompt

Language Comprehension

- Check the children are reading with phrasing and expression.

- Ask the children what the instructions tell them to make here.

- Ask the children what is the first thing they need to do to make the monster's body.

- What do the children think they will be told how to make next?

Tuning In

Now what will you make?

What is the hair made from?

Observe and Prompt

Word Recognition

- If the children have difficulty reading 'Eyes' and 'Hair', help them with these words.

- If the children have difficulty reading 'buttons' and 'cotton', prompt them to break each word down into two syllables, before blending the whole word together.

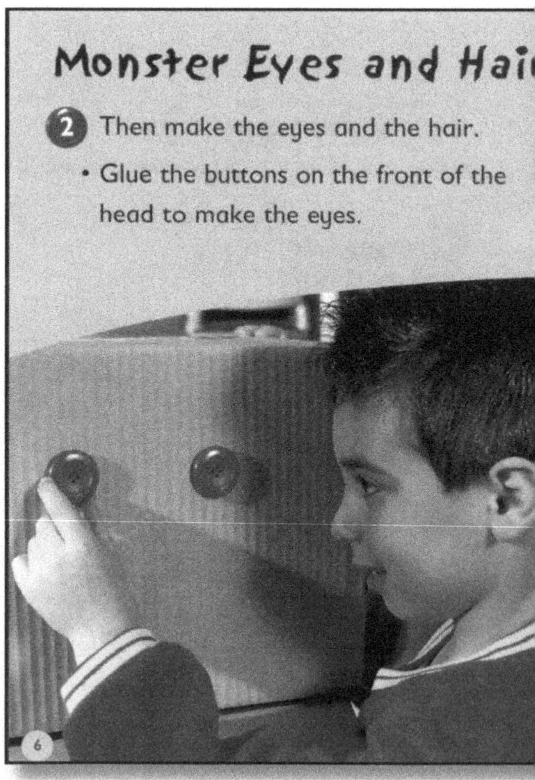

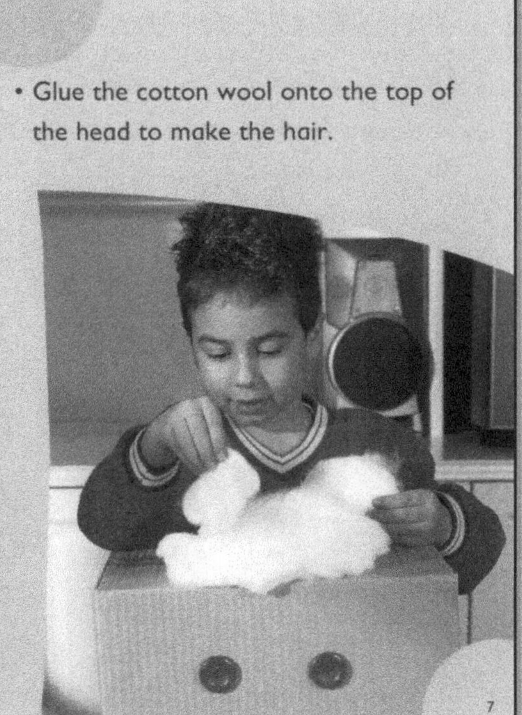

• Glue the cotton wool onto the top of the head to make the hair.

 **Observe and Prompt**

Language Comprehension

- Check the children have located all the text on the page.

- Check the children are reading with appropriate phrasing, taking notice of punctuation.

- Ask the children what they need to use to make the monster's eyes.

Tuning In

Where will you stick the cups?

What is the nose made from?

 ## Observe and Prompt

Word Recognition

- Check the children are using their decoding skills to read 'Ears'. Help them with the 'ear' sound if they struggle.

- If the children have difficulty reading 'scouring', model the blending of this word for them, emphasising the 'our' sound.

8

- Stick the scouring pad on the front of the head to make the nose.

 ## Observe and Prompt

Language Comprehension

- Ask the children what the text tells them to make now.

- Ask the children what they need to use for the nose. Do they know what this object is?

- What do the children think the text will tell them to make next?

Tuning In

Now what will the boy add to the face?

How do you think he has made the eyebrows?

Observe and Prompt

Word Recognition

- If the children have difficulty reading 'Eyebrows', model the blending of this word for them.

- If the children have difficulty reading 'triangles', prompt them to break the word down into three syllables, before blending the whole word together. Help the children with the 'le' sound at the end of this word if they struggle.

- Check the children are using their decoding skills to tackle the more difficult words on these pages (e.g. 'Draw', 'paint', 'mouth').

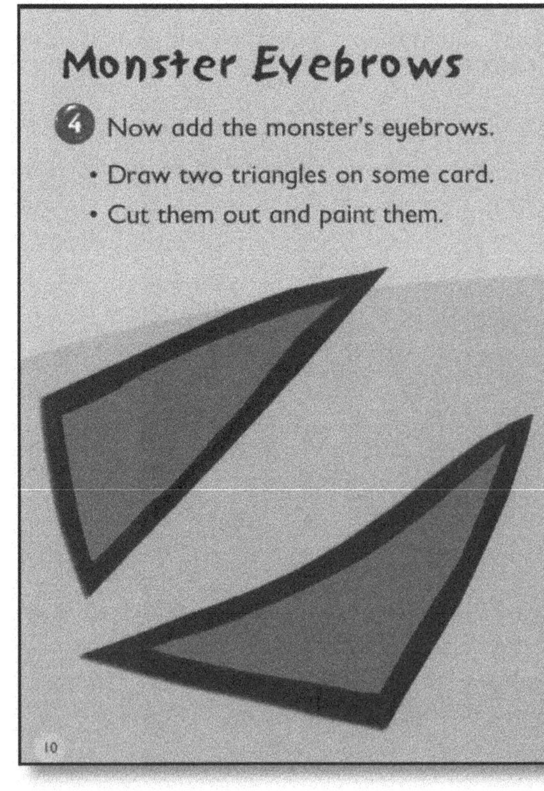

10

Tuning In

What is the mouth made from?

 **Observe and Prompt**

Language Comprehension

- Check the children can identify and read the headings.

- Ask the children what the boy has used to make the eyebrows.

- Do the children think the monster's mouth looks frightening?

 **Tuning In**

What will you need to make the hands and feet?

 **Observe and Prompt**

Word Recognition

- Prompt the children to break the word 'decorate' down into three syllables, before blending the whole word together.

- If the children have difficulty reading 'Finally', model the blending of this word for them.

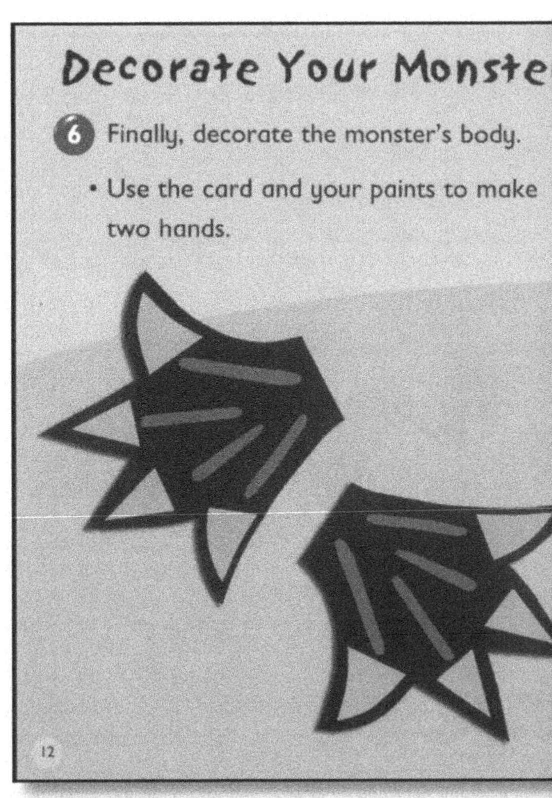

 **Observe and Prompt**

Language Comprehension

- Ask the children what the final instructions are on these pages.

- Ask the children what they need to use to make the monster's feet.

- Do the children think the monster is nearly ready?

Tuning In

Where do you think you glue the hands, feet and clothes?

 **Observe and Prompt**

Word Recognition

- If the children have difficulty reading 'Finish', prompt them to break the word down into two syllables, before blending the whole word together.
- Check the children can read 'Your' and 'You've' using their decoding skills.

Finish Your Monster

- Glue the hands, feet and clothes to the front of the body.

Well done! You've made a monster

14

Language Comprehension

- Check that the children are reading all the text on the page.

- Ask the children if they think the monster is finished now.

- Do the children think it is a good monster?

Tuning In

What other monsters could you make?

 ## Observe and Prompt

Word Recognition

- Check the children can read 'other' using their decoding skills.
- Check the children can read the sight word 'could'.

 ## Observe and Prompt

Language Comprehension

- Check the children are reading with expression and phrasing, taking notice of the punctuation.
- Ask the children if they want to try making a monster.
- What other things do the children like making?